THE MIDDLE AGES

A Medieval Pageant For Your Classroom

by

ELIZABETH MARTEN
NINA CROSBY

Illustrations by Susan Kondziela

Cover .... "Our Stained Glass Window"

Page 4 ...... "Guild Banners"

Page 6 ...... "Teachers At Work"

Page 20 ..... "A Medieval Fair"

Page 23 ..... "A Medieval Scribe"

Page 33 ..... "Shoemaker, Hatterer, Smithy
                            & Armorer"

Page 49 ..... "The Alchemist"

Page 57 ..... "A Leisured Afternoon"

ISBN 0-914634-90-9

© 1986
D.O.K. PUBLISHERS
EAST AURORA, NY 14052

Contents

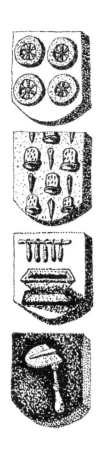

Overview

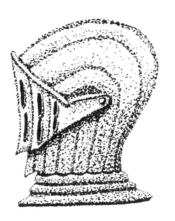

The Middle Ages enables students to explore history and gain an understanding of what has gone on before while mastering basic skills. The unit of study gets away from the routine of class discussion, report writing, and recall questions so often used in our classrooms. It contains a series of directed activities that encourage students to read widely and explore this time period. Students are involved in skills development activities and encouraged to apply these skills to areas interesting them. The primary goals of the study are:

1. To extend and enrich basic skills.
2. To develop awareness of historical events and their relationship to modern life.
3. To strengthen the relationship between school and community through cooperative planning.

This unit of study addresses these established goals by providing students with activities designed to develop skills areas particularly in the Language Arts and the Social Sciences. In depth exploration of historical events builds awareness. A well planned fair or festival solidifies school and community relationships.

A classroom Renaissance Festival or Medieval Fair is the focal point of the unit. Asterisked student activities are recommended as projects that lead to the production of a fair or festival in your classroom. Students are involved in explorations of history as per individual interest. Sample forms developed in the original pilot are included as are numerous student worksheets. These should serve to stimulate ideas. Changes should be made to suit individual classroom and student needs.

The Middle Ages provides a flexible framework which allows for teacher and student input and creativity. It is important to remember that this unit of study can and should be modified to meet the needs of students involved and to reflect the community resources available in each school setting.

Parents, students, and mentors, as well as school personnel, should be involved in evaluation activities. Sample forms for evaluation have been included to suggest ways of insuring evaluative data from each group. In addition, certain selected activities may be selected for skills and performance evaluation of students. As a convenience, a pre/post test form is also included in the materials.

To facilitate planning the following materials have been included for teacher and student use:

-A Proposed Time Schedule
-Sample Forms
-Teacher Notes
-Analogies Worksheets

-Pre/Post Test Sample
-Activities by Discipline
-Student Activities keyed to Bloom

Teacher Notes

The Middle Ages is a term employed to identify the period in time in European History between Ancient and Modern times. The term applies to a period of history with indefinite beginning and end. The exact period of the Middle Age varies with the resource. Therefore, exact dates will not be given to identify the span of the unit of instruction. It does, however, develop concepts from Medieval times through the Renaissance. Skills development in this unit of study focuses on these areas:

--Reading in the Content Areas
--Skimming for information
--Notetaking/Outlining/Bibliographies
--Oral and Written Reporting
--Vocabulary Development

An extension of this unit can be made by including the unit Don't Teach! Let Me Learn About Shakespeare, D.O.K., Buffalo, NY (C) 1979. The Shakespeare study adds a dimension of literature with a focus on comprehension and interpretive reading.

Reading in the Content areas is a primary focus of this unit of study. Students should be guided to read historical references for comprehension. Guided reading lessons may be structured to help students determine importance and relevance of content. You as the teacher may select specific background activities to help teach this particular reading skill. Students should be assisted in establishing questions to be answered in their reading. What is it that you want to know? What resources may be useful in providing such information?

Assist your students in becoming capable, independent readers. Setting purposes for reading is important as in any reading lesson. It is necessary for student questions to focus at all levels of Bloom's Taxonomy to provide the necessary challenge desired for gifted students.

Many of the unit activities require students to use library resources and skim for information. You may want to structure one or more lessons to teach students to skim for information. Students should be aware that in research-related activities they may find skimming a necessary and useful skill. Remember that skimming means reading rapidly through material to locate the main idea or answer to a specific question. When finding answers to questions that ask "What", "Who", "Where", and "When" answers can usually be found by skimming. Guide students to read more carefully to answer "How" and "Why" questions.

Review or teach these guidelines for skimming information with your students:

Use the index and table of contents to find specific entries.

Look for topic or subtopics to locate necessary information.

Watch for key words and phrases that are related to the topic or question.

Read materials as rapidly as possible to find the needed answer.

Make necessary notes to answer questions.

Notetaking is another special skill that may be developed in this unit of study. As students skim for information related to their questions and topics, they will need to rely heavily on accurate notetaking. Students should understand that notetaking is a brief way of summarizing or condensing important information. Students must be encouraged not to copy long reference passages, but rather to make brief important notes and references related to their topic. Notes must be clear and meaningful. These notes will need to be translated into the students' own words in answering questions and developing projects.

Notes from several sources may be combined to provide more complete answers to problems posed. At this point, you may want to teach or review outlining skills. Outlining should be reinforced as it is taught in the students' regular English program, however, the most common outline is as follows:

    I. Main Topic or Idea
        A. Supporting fact
            1. Detail
            2. Detail
        B. Supporting fact
   II. Main topic or idea

Because this unit of study requires students to use multiple references and to record information from these references, it also is a suitable time to develop skills in writing bibliographies. Students should include bibliographic data on note cards. This should be taught in the form accepted by the advanced level English classes in each school system. One widely accepted bibliographical entry form for books is this one:

Sherwood, Merrian, The Song of Roland, Macmillan, 1946; pp.

Students may also need acceptable forms for interview, periodicals. You may find these examples useful:

Sullivan, Sandra, personal interview, January 3, 19 .

Boothe, Rose, "A Classroom Camelot", Teacher Magazine, January 1978, pp. 98 - 100.

Colliers' Encyclopedia, "Renaissance", Vol. 19, (C) 1963, pp. 723 - 735.

The nature of this study requires students to read, gather information and prepare both oral and written reports. These suggestions may be useful in guiding students to preparation of successful reports.

Plan reports carefully. Key or guide questions will serve as guidelines for main topics in the final report.

Research should fill in the supporting facts and details.

Information should be arranged in a logical sequence.

Keep the report interesting by using quotations and anecdotes.

Direct conversation or quotations may add interest to a report.

Written reports should be in your best handwriting or typewritten for neatness.

Proofread written reports. Check for spelling and punctuation errors. Does your writing make sense? Are ideas complete?

Written reports and oral reports are prepared in much the same manner. However, there are some additional considerations for preparing good oral reports and presentations. These suggestions may be useful to your students:

Practice oral reports before a mirror, with a friend or someone at home.

Consider the rate at which you speak. Keep the pace slow enough so that it's easy for your audience to understand.

Speak loudly enough so that you can be heard clearly.

Consider visual or audio-visual aids that might help develop ideas. Could you use posters, charts, films, or other materials to help make ideas clear and interesting?

Tell your information. Don't read it. You may want to speak from notes, but reading word for word tends to be dull.

Remember these are general guidelines for successful reports. You may want to add, modify, change, or eliminate any of these suggestions as you develop expectations for your students.

Vocabulary development is evident throughout the unit. Many vocabulary words have been identified with specific instructions for development. You may find additional words and terms you want students to know. As these are identified, plan for their development. Asking students to keep personal vocabulary notebooks is useful. Individuals then may be encouraged to make entries as they encounter difficulties. A personalized approach to vocabulary development is highly desirable.

Unit activities also provide for individual interests and abilities. These activities should be assigned as needed or desired for students dependent on their individual strengths and weaknesses. Provisions have been made for creative expression. Activities involving art, music, and drama are evident. Creative writing and role playing activities encourage students to develop self expression.

Developmental and creative activities provide maximum flexibility in assigning or selecting individual and group tasks to be completed. This flexibility allows potential for maximum student learning success.

TEACHER REFERENCES

Age of Western Expansion, Allyn and Bacon, Boston, 1975.

Medieval Civilization, Allyn and Bacon, Boston, 1975

"A Classroom Camelot," Teacher, January 1978, pp. 98-100. (Author: Rose Boothe)

"Shakespeare and Company: The Best in Classroom Reading and Drama," The Reading Teacher, January 1980, pp. 438 - 441. (Author: Carol Cox)

THE MIDDLE AGES . . . .

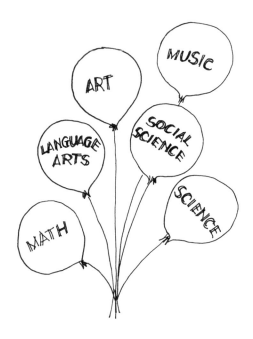

MULTIDISCIPLINARY IN NATURE.

— Activities include all basic curricular areas.

— Activities allow for flexibility in setting goals for individual students or student groups.

— Activities provide for skills development in all areas with concentration in Language Arts and Social Studies.

— Activities are identifed by discipline.

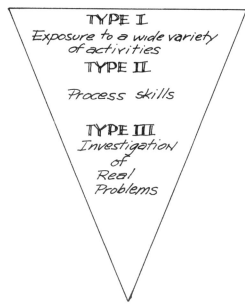

STRUCTURED TO PROVIDE ACTIVITIES AT ALL LEVELS OF RENZULLI'S ENRICHMENT TRIAD

— Activities provide exposure to areas of interest and varied experiences not ordinarily offered in the regular curriculum.

— Skills in research, creativity, problem solving, work/study, and effective development are taught through guided activities.

— Activities permit individual students to focus on a particular interest and develop in depth knowledge of a particular area.

— Developmental workshops are included for activities marked with a "W".

A COLLECTION OF ACTIVITIES REPRESENTING ALL LEVELS OF BLOOM'S TAXONOMY OF COGNITIVE THINKING.

— Activity levels provide for individualization so students may develop as they are able.

— Student activities are coded to aid student/teacher planning.

— A broad choice of activity types provides increased flexibility in both heterogenous and homogenous settings.

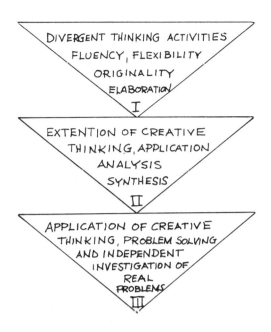

COMPATIBLE WITH TREFFINGER'S TRIAD MODEL FOR CREATIVE LEARNING.

— Brainstorming activites are included.

— Activities are coded to show those appropriate for application, analysis, and synthesis.

— Student projects allow for development of fluency, flexibility, originality and elaborateness.

— Choice activities provide for independent investigation.

— The Middle Ages lets students get a "real" look at history.

THE MIDDLE AGES INVOLVES EVERYONE!

THE TEACHER

— Becomes a facilitator of learning.

— Carefully plans and coordinates activities.

— Uses resourcefulness to obtain help from other school staff, parents, and mentors.

— Guides students in required and selected activity choices to meet individual needs.

— Keeps all groups informed as the unit progresses.

— Maintains careful records for evaluation and possible replication.

— Makes festival preparations well in advance.
— Keeps parents and members well informed.

— Collects wide variety of resource materials for student use.

— Makes necessary arrangements with administrators, including preliminary plans, reports, and final evaluations.

THE PARENTS

— Appreciate being included in the planning and progress reporting.
— Must understand the intended goals and objectives of the study.
— Can provide guidance for their students helping them to keep on target with independent study projects.
— Must give permission for field experience as with any other trip.
— Can be valuable resources in identifying mentors, serving as mentors, and arranging transportation.
— May have suggestions for improving the study.
— Can provide volunteer help to monitor small group activities.
— Should be included in culmination and evaluation activities.

THE MENTORS

— Can direct and share specific knowledge to particular students or student groups.
— Are a vital part of the program.
— Strengthen relationships between the school and community through cooperative planning.
— Provide one-to-one field experience giving needed attention to each child.
— Should have advanced information about the student with whom they are partnered.
— Should have clearly established roles and responsibilities.
— Should be involved in culmination and evaluation activities.

THE STUDENTS

— Are involved in group study and planning.
— Have the opportunity to focus on personal interests.
— Are taught basic skills which are reinforced through application.
— Are exposed to a broad base of materials, activities, and experiences.
— Receive attention based on individual interest as well as strengths and weaknesses.
— Develop an appreciation of history and historical contributions.
— Learn to assume responsibility for their work and their actions.
— Gain self-esteem.
— Gain a sense of self-direction.
— Learn the need for cooperating with others.
— Should be involved in evaluation activities.

MANAGEMENT PLAN

Syllabus	Teacher and School Personnel	Parents	Mentors and Volunteers	Students
EXPLORATORY FIRST WEEK ACTIVITIES AND MOTIVATION	— Obtain administrative consent — Secure help and cooperation from other staff members and Library Personnel	— Inform parents of the plan for this unit of study		— Pretest — Introduce motivational activities — Spark student interest through cooperative planning
EXPLORATORY ACTIVITIES SECOND WEEK	— Establish Learning Centers — Evaluate skills needs of the group and individual student	— Assist students in selecting independent study activities — Help to provide resources for student to use	— Guest speakers — Resource persons — Story tellers	— Literature Activities — Background Reading — Complete individual — Student/Teacher Contract — Indentify needed resource — Vocabulary Building
THIRD WEEK	— Guide students in developing individual contracts — Facilitate wide use of resources	— Help students learn to budget time and complete tasks.		
INTRODUCE CULMINATING PROJECT	— Decide on format for pageant, fair or festival — Consider possible times — Consider possible locations — Introduce outline of idea to students for planning — Monitor student progress on contract tasks. — Maintain communication with parents, mentors, and volunteers.	— Involvement in planning culminating activity — Providing resources and assistance for individual student projects	— Assistance with small groups — Technical Assistance	— Complete assigned tasks — Planning of culminating activity — Independent work
FIFTH WEEK	— Finalize plans for pageant, fair or festival — Guide students in necessary tasks for production — Determine audience			— Write skits — Plan costumes — Decide sequence of events — Create necessary props, scenery — Make arrangements for advertising
SIXTH WEEK CULMINATION	— Practice scenes for pageant, fair or festival — Make last minute changes — Confirm arrangements involving others	— Guide students in completing projects — Make suggestions — Provide assistance and resources for production	— Technical Assistance	— Practice for pageant, fair or festival — Make necessary changes — Make costumes — Advertise — Extend special invitations — Print programs
EVALUATION	— Evaluate student contracts — Evaluate student performance in groups — Evaluate student skills growth — Final report to administration and parents	— Evaluate learning via students participation	— Evaluate participation with teacher and students	— Evaluate self-learning — Evaluate performance — Evaluate total program

STUDENT RESPONSIBILITY SHEET

As the culmination to our study of the Middle Ages, we plan to present a pageant (or festival or fair). Each student must assume part of the reponsibility to make the total project a success.

_____ is working to prepare a scene or demonstration
    student

entitled _____. The program will be held _____
                                                                        date

at _____. Activities will begin promptly at _____
        location   time

and last until _____.
                  time

Transportation Arrangements:

Costume:

Props/Scenery:

Student Responsibility:

Special Information:

Please review your child's responsibilities. If there are any problems, please call me at school.

                            Teacher's Name _____
                            Telephone Number

_____

I have reviewed my child's responsibilities for the Middle Ages project.

_____ has my permission to accept this assignment.
    student

Comments:

                            _____
14   Parent/Guardian

PARENT EVALUATION

Were the plans for the (pageant, fair, festival) clear and understandable?

_____

Did the Student Responsibility Sheet provide useful information?

_____

What additional information would have been useful or of interest?

_____

What was your child's reaction to the unit of study? _____

_____

What was your child's reaction to the (pageant, fair, festival)? _____

_____

What was your reaction to the unit? _____

_____

What was your reaction to the (pageant, fair, festival)? _____

_____

COMMENTS:

_____
Parent

STUDENT EVALUATION

What did you like best about the unit? _____

_____ Why? _____

_____

What did you like the least? _____

_____ Why? _____

_____

Did you use your time wisely? _____

How could the unit have been improved? _____

_____

How could you evaluate the (pageant, fair, festival)? _____

_____

Did you do your part to make it successful? _____

_____

COMMENTS:

MENTOR'S EVALUATION

Were the pre-classroom preparations sufficient for the task you were asked to
do? _____

What was your reaction to the time spent with the child/children? _____

_____

_____

What changes would you suggest for future planning? _____

_____

Would you be willing to be involved in other school related projects? _____

_____

May we add your name to our school reference file? _____

_____   _____
            Name   Address

_____
            Phone

Areas of interest: _____

_____

_____

17

PRETEST - POST TEST

Select the proper term from the list below.

abbott	moat	moveable type	cathedrals	musician
vassal	joust	printing	dungeon	squire
cloister	craftsman	castles	builder	keep

1. A water filled ditch around the outside of a castle is called a _____.

2. The covered walkway around a monastery is known as a _____.

3. The most beautiful and important buildings constructed during the Middle Ages were the _____.

4. Leonardo da Vinci was a famous painter, but he also was a _____ as well as a _____.

5. The most important invention during the Middle Ages was that of _____.

Read the questions. Circle the letter indicating the correct answer.

1. Each town in the Middle Ages was protected by a
   a. wall   c. king
   b. road   d. guard

2. Skilled craftsmen protected their business and trade by forming

   a. unions   c. armies
   b. guilds   d. companies

3. A boy who wanted to learn a trade must first work as

   a. a craftsman   c. an apprentice
   b. a journeyman   d. a guide

4. Tournaments were held

   a. for fun   c. to gain power
   b. to practice fighting   d. to defend one's honor

5. A lord's castle was primarily important

   a. as a place of beauty   c. to house one's wealth
   b. as a place for comfortable living d. as a defense

In your own words, complete these thoughts.

1. The stories told by Marco Polo stirred people of Europe to _____

    _____

    _____

2. The invention of gunpowder put an end to feudalism because _____

    _____

    _____

3. Gutenberg's press revolutionized modern life because _____

    _____

    _____

4. Feudalism is _____

    _____

5. The time called the Middle Ages ended with the Renaissance. The word
    Renaissance means _____

    _____

NOTE: This is a sample test. Questions may be changed or additions made to
coincide with the study topics chosen by teacher and students.

A Pageant or Fair

A pageant or fair is a suitable culmination for this unit of study. Hosting a Renaissance Festival is an exciting and challenging way for students to organize information learned and share it with others. Students should understand that a pageant requires planning and hard work. Several weeks should be allowed for such a project.

Students should understand that a pageant is somewhat like a play, but usually has more scenes. Music, dancing, acting and speaking are combined to develop short scenes to create the desired feelings. Everyone in the group can be included in developing a pageant about life in the Middle Ages. Students should play an active part in determining which scenes should be included and exactly how they should be presented. It might be helpful to have students follow these steps in planning a pageant.

Step 1 - Complete group and independent research to build a foundation for the project. All students should have mastered basic information about the Middle Ages.

Understanding is the basis for sound planning. Students should be encouraged to read widely to find their own ideas for pageant scenes.

Step 2 - List possible topics to be developed as pageant scenes. The list of ideas should be brainstormed freely. Perhaps an on-going chart can be developed. Each entry on the list should be evaluated for importance and ease of production. Those that are considered important should be transferred to a production list.

Step 3 - Each subject or event identified for development should be assigned to a particular student or student group for additional research and development. The first task might be to construct a clear, concise paragraph describing the subject or event. The ideas expressed in the paragraphs should provide information and guidance necessary in developing pageant scenes.

Step 4 - Decide what should happen in each scene. Outline the scene carefully. Assign parts and practice speeches that you think tell the story. Ask other classmates to evaluate your scene and make suggestions for improving it. Modify the scene to make it as good as possible.

Step 5 - Decide on costumes, props, and scenery. Keep your "extras" simple. The more complex your scenes become, the more difficult they are to produce. Use simple materials to create the effect that you feel is important. Be creative!

Step 6 - Ask others to make suggestions for improving your pageant. Consult your music teachers, art teachers, etc. Perhaps someone in your school or community can help plan dances to be included. Consider other resource people who might be able to give advice and help.

Step 7 - Decide on the proper sequence of scenes in your pageant. You might think of the events on time line. Keeping ideas in time line order usually makes it easier for others to understand. If you plan scenes out of time order, be certain you have good reasons.

Step 8 - Design a program for your pageant. Include scenes, titles, participants, credits, drawings, and any other important information. You may want to include short poems or writings developed during the unit. Remember to keep the flavor of the Middle Ages. Consider the work of the scribes and early printers.

Step 9 - Decide on the time, location, and audience for your pageant. You may need to make special arrangements to hold your pageant at the desired time and in the best location.

Step 10 - Issue invitations and/or advertise your pageant. Knowing who you want for an audience will help you decide on how to handle invitations and advertising. If you use invitations, it might be desirable to write them on rolls as the books written by scribes were written. If you desire a larger open audience you may want to extend some special personal invitations and then advertise for a large audience. Advertising may be done with posters, radio ads, and television spots. It may be announced in school newsletters and community newspapers. Investigate media that announce community happenings free of charge. Find out how their materials should be prepared. Follow the rules to get the best possible coverage. Also be sure that your advertisements are accurately prepared. Remember only high quality work should go before the public. Check for misspellings, messiness and other careless errors. Make certain that information is accurate and easy to understand.

A Middle Ages Fair or Renaissance Festival might be conducted and would also follow pageant guidelines. The difference would be that a festival or fair would take place in a large area with several different things going on at once. Your audience may come and go. They also may move freely from one scene or happening to another. In planning a fair or festival consider these questions:

1. What space is available?
2. What events might occur at the same times?
3. What scenes or events can be repeated easily?
4. What special events need to be planned and particular times announced?
5. How long should your festival or fair last?

Plan your festival or fair to include everyone. Each person should take responsibility for his part in the success of the project. Plan carefully with your students and other personnel in your school and community. Include parents and relatives in your plans. They may be able to suggest ways to help make this project better and often can help with special projects.

Before beginning a special project such as a fair or festival you will need to seek the approval of the building administrator and others who may be involved in decision making regarding the project. Confirm space and time arrangements. Make any other necessary plans that will make the project run more smoothly.

You will find it useful to maintain close communication with parents during the development of the unit. Keeping parents informed helps to establish open communication. Many times you will find willing helpers when parents are aware of the scope of the project.

Activities that might be suitable for development into pageant or festival projects are asterisked. These notations serve only as a guide. Encourage students to develop their own ideas for scenes and happenings. You as the teacher can guide selection and encourage creative adaptation.

Additional activities can be found in Don't Teach! Let Me Learn About Shakespeare, D.O.K., Buffalo, NY, 1979. Many activities from Shakespeare are suitable for inclusion in a pageant, fair or festival.

Language Arts

LANGUAGE ARTS

UNIT MATRIX

ACTIVITY	Knowledge	Comprehension	Application	Analysis	Synthesis	Evaluation
1	X			X	X	X
2				X		X
3			X	X	X	
4	X					
5	X	X				
6		X		X	X	
7	X					
8				X		X
9		X	X			
10			X	X.	X	
11	X	X				
12		X			X	
13			X	X	X	
14		X		X	X	
15				X	X	
16				X	X	
17	X	X				
18	X	X				
19		X		X		
20		X		X		X
21	X	X				
22		X	X	X	X	
23	X	X				
24	X	X				
25			X	X	X	
26				X	X	
27		X		X	X	
28		X	X			
29					X	
30		X	X		X	
31		X	X		X	
32		X	X			

Bloom's Taxonomy

* 1. BE A JESTER

OBJECTIVE: K, An, S, E

Jesters were very popular during the Middle Ages.
What kinds of performances did they give? Why were
they popular with the people? Can you plan a jester's routine and perform it? Does your audience
find the act funny? How could you improve your
performance?

3. FAMOUS FABLES

OBJECTIVE: Ap, An, S

Peasants and townspeople liked stories about ani-
mals. An old fable that was written down during
the Middle Ages was called "Reynard, the Fox."
Find this story in your library. Read it. What
kind of story is a fable? Can you find other stories of the same type? Were they written during the
same time period? Can you write a new animal tale
using the same period?

* 5. LEARNING LEGENDS

OBJECTIVE: K, C

Wandering singers and storytellers told adventures
of brave knights. Some of these legends were written down. In England, these stories were those of
Arthur and the Knights of the Round Table. Read
some of the tales. Write a new tale of your own.

7. THE PRINTERS

OBJECTIVE: K

John Fust and William Caxton were Renaissance printers. Each of them make a contribution to modern
printing. Can you name what each contributed?

2. THE WORD

OBJECTIVE: An, E

During the Middle Ages, there was a rise of new language, not only Latin was spoken. Books began to be written in other languages. What affect would the change have on the world? What changes would this bring about?

4. VOCABULARY BUILDING

OBJECTIVE: K

These vocabulary words will be useful to you in your study. Learn the definitions and be able to use each in a sentence.

Renaissance	mortuary	knight	page
feudalism	gauntlet	crusade	lord
apprentice	squire	joust	shrew
protestant	tallage	abbot	moat
navigation	jesuit	peasant	serf
medieval	cloister	Gothic	title

6. A SUITABLE SATIRE

OBJECTIVE: C, An, S

Study the story of Don Quixote. This is considered a satire. It makes fun of or ridicules life in the Middle Ages. Show your understanding of satire by pointing out satirical statements or ideas in this work. Go one step further! Write a satire of your own.

8. BEGINNING BOOKS

OBJECTIVE: An, E

Books have always been important to man. This is one way to convey information to others. At first, the only books were handwritten in Latin by Monks. A Monk could only copy a couple of books in a year's time. What did this do to the value of books? Who could own these? How did this method of producing books affect the growth of knowledge?

9. ORNAMENTAL SCRIPT

OBJECTIVE: C, Ap

Monks who copied books took great pride in their
work. They developed beautiful handwriting skills.
They also decorate the beginning letters on each
page. These letters were often, large, fancy, and
in a variety of colors. Investigate in your library
to find examples of this style.

11. WHO'S WHO

OBJECTIVE: K, C

Select one of the following people to study carefully. Use several sources to investigate the life
of the person you select. Write a factual report
in the form of a biographical sketch.

Prince Henry of Portugal	Martin Luther	Raphael
Ignatius Loyola	Gutenberg	da Vinci
William Caxton	John Calvin	John Fust
Michalangelo	Marco Polo	Homer

* 13. BALLADS AND VERSES

OBJECTIVE: Ap, An, S

Ballads were a popular verse form. Can you find
examples of ballads? Did any of these originate
in the Middle Ages? Can you identify modern ballads? Write a ballad of your own.

15. CREATE A HERO

OBJECTIVE: An, S

Create a new literary hero who might have lived in
the Middle Ages. Write a story or book about the
adventures of your new hero. Keep the setting and
historical events as accurate as possible.

10. THE ODDESSY

OBJECTIVE: Ap, An, S

The Epic was a popular study of literature during the Middle Ages. What is an epic? The Oddessy written by Homer was printed during the fifteenth century and became popular reading. It is still widely read. Read this epic. How does it fit the definition of an epic? Can you find other literary examples of epic writing?   Perhaps you will want to write an epic of your own.

12. STUDY THE STYLE

OBJECTIVE: C, S

Study these literary styles and tell something about each of them. Select one literary style and write a composition using that style to relate information about the Middle Ages.

Fiction	Satire	Essay
Legend	Ballad	Epic

* 14. HERO TALES

OBJECTIVE: C, An, E

Hero tales such as those of Robin Hood were popular stories of the times. Read several stories about Robin Hood. How would you describe the character Robin Hood portrays? Can you identify the forces of good and evil? How do you feel about Robin Hood's actions? Write a Robin Hood tale of your own.

16. YOU, THE ARTIST

OBJECTIVE: An, S

Pretend that you are a Renaissance artist such as Michalangelo or da Vinci. Try your hand at producing paintings or sculptures with a Renaissance style. Can you model the work of these artists giving attention to the same qualities? Exhibit your work in a one-man show or invite others to join you and create a classroom museum.

17. HALF-N-HALF

OBJECTIVE: K, C

Read the Song of Roland or parts of it. It is said to be half truth and half legend. Explain this statement.

* 19. NURSERY RHYME HISTORY

OBJECTIVE: C, An

Remember the Nursery rhyme "Simple Simon met a pieman"? Find the rhyme and read it carefully. How might the rhyme indicate that Simple Simon and the pieman lived during the Middle Ages. Perhaps you will want to plan for a pieman at your pageant or festival. How would he dress? What would he sell?

21. TIME LINE

OBJECTIVE: K, C

Trace changes and developments in printing from Gutenberg's moveable type to present. Discuss how printing improvements affect life, knowledge, etc.

23. A FIRST

OBJECTIVE: K, C

The first book of any size to be printed with moveable type came from a press owned by John Gutenberg in 1456. What book was this? Where is it located today? Can you estimate its value?

* 18. BEOWULF

OBJECTIVE: K, C

Read the story of Beowulf. How does this story
reflect the beliefs of the Middle Ages? If you
were a Bard or storyteller, how would you relate
the story of Beowulf to your listeners?

20. A GIANT STEP IN PRINTING

OBJECTIVE: C, An, E

Moveable type was a giant step forward in printing and book making. Explain how moveable type
presses revolutionized the world of literature.
How did moveable type change the printing world?

22. TELL IT IN PICTURES

OBJECTIVE: C, Ap, An, S

Select one of the many subjects in this study and
create a picture sequence to tell the story. For
example, use pictures to show the Crusades, the
adventures of Marco Polo, the first voyage of Columbus, the work of a Renaissance artist, etc. Arrange them in a book or make a mural.

* 24. HOW TO'S

OBJECTIVE: K, C

Explain the operation of Gutenberg's press. Use
charts, diagrams, or pictures to help make your
explanation clear.

25. EXTRA! EXTRA!

OBJECTIVE: Ap, An, S

Write a headline and the accompanying news article
telling about some special or grand event at a
particular castle.

27. LEARN FROM ADAM

OBJECTIVE: C, An, S

Adam of the Road by Elizabeth Janet Gray is a famous story set in the Middle Ages. Read the book.
How do the circumstances of the Middle Ages effect
Adam and the story? Would the story change if the
setting changed? Explain. Perhaps you will want
to rewrite Adam of the Road in a modern setting.

29. ONCE UPON A TIME

OBJECTIVE: S

Write an original story or book with Middle Ages
setting and characters. Try using Old English
for certain words. Use your best style to scribe
your story. Illustrate your book showing appropriate scenery and clothing.

31. A CRUSADER

OBJECTIVE: C, Ap, S

Pretend that you are a member of the Crusades
forces. Write an account of your life as a
participant in the Crusades. Give your re-
actions, evaluations, and hopes at this time.
Describe your experiences and surroundings.
You might prepare your report on parchment.

31

26. HEAR YE! HEAR YE!

OBJECTIVE: An, S

Parchment rolls were used for communication. Prepare messages on parchment. What might they say?
Who might they be from? For whom are they intended?

28. ST. FRANCIS OF ASSISI

OBJECTIVE: C, Ap

You may want to research the life of St. Francis
of Assisi. What was his work? Why did he seem
to have great influence on his people? How is
St. Francis pictured today? Can you find repre-
sentations and pictures? How do these show the
kind of person St. Francis must have been? You
may want to read Higher than the Arrow by Judy
VantlerVeer. This is a modern story about St.
Francis and will show how his influence has
spanned generations.

* 30. THE LITERATURE

OBJECTIVE: C, Ap, S

Read The Trumpeter of Krakow by Eric P. Kelly.
Make notes of the details the author uses to
create the feeling of the Middle Ages. Perhaps
your class would be able to make this story into
a play.

32. PRETTY PRINT

OBJECTIVE: C, Ap

Investigate the art of Calligraphy. What is it?
Research the topic. Demonstrate your understanding by creating a display of various examples of
calligraphy.

Social Science

33

SOCIAL SCIENCE

UNIT MATRIX

ACTIVITY	Knowledge	Comprehension	Application	Analysis	Synthesis	Evaluation
1				X	X	
2				X	X	
3		X	X			
4			X	X	X	
5	X		X			
6				X		X
7			X	X		
8			X	X		
9			X	X		
10		X	X	X		
11	X	X	X			
12			X	X		
13		X				
14			X	X	X	
15		X	X			
16		X				X
17		X				
18	X	X				
19	X	X				
20		X		X		
21		X		X	X	
22		X				
23				X	X	
24		X	X			
25			X	X		
26				X		X
27		X		X	X	
28	X				X	

ACTIVITY	Knowledge	Comprehension	Application	Analysis	Synthesis	Evaluation
29	X					
30				X	X	X
31				X	X	X
32				X		X
33			X			
34		X	X			
35			X		X	
36		X	X			
37				X		X
38			X			
39	X	X				
40	X	X				
41		X	X		X	
42					X	
43		X	X			
44		X			X	
45		X	X			
46		X			X	
47		X		X		X
48	X	X	X			
49		X	X			
50			X	X		
51		X	X			
52		X	X			
53			X			
54			X			
55	X	X				
56				X	X	X

Bloom's Taxonomy

1. YOUR TOWN

OBJECTIVE: An, S

Imagine you live in a European town during the
Middle Ages. What does your town look like?
Who lives there with you? What work goes on
there? Consider other details. Now imagine
that you can break the time barrier. Write a
letter to tell your friend in Modern America
what life in your town is like.

* 3. USING THE MEDIA

OBJECTIVE: C, Ap

Select one of these topics and plan a short doc-
umentary. You may want to produce a short television program, make your own filmstrip, or create a paper-roll film. No matter what the media,
stick closely to your topic. Here are your choices:

Life in a Monastery   Life in a Castle
Life in a Serf Village   Life as a Master Craftsman

* 5. COMMUNITY CHANGES

OBJECTIVE: K, Ap

One of the most important changes toward the end
of the Renaissance was the move from castle villages to market towns. Explain the differences.
Perhaps you could make pictures, murals, or even
dramas to show the changes that occured late in
the Middle Ages.

7. LEARNING A TRADE

OBJECTIVE: Ap, An

In the craft guilds, new trainees moved through
planned training steps. First one became an apprentice, then a journeyman, and finally, a master workman. Explain each level of training.
Compare this plan with training programs offered to modern craftsmen.

35

* 2. FESTIVAL OR FAIR?

OBJECTIVE: An, S

During the Middle Ages a town might hold a market
or fair. How did a town get permission to hold
these events? What was the difference between a
market and a fair? Make a mural or a table top
display to show events of a market or fair.

4. BARTER AND TRADE

OBJECTIVE: Ap, An, S

In the castle villages of the Middle Ages, people
had to produce materials to satisfy their own needs.
Men in the villages became expert weavers, shoemakers,
and carpenters. They spent most of their time producing the special items or product. They traded these
products for others that they needed. Explain how this
bartering system caused changes in the Middle Ages. How
does this system compare with the economic system as we
know it today?

6. UNDERSTANDING MEANINGS

OBJECTIVE: An, E

Renaissance means "rebirth" or "awakening". Explain
why this period of time at the conclusion of the Middle Ages was aptly called the Renaissance.

8. GUILDS AND YOUR STREETS

OBJECTIVE: Ap, An

Members of the craft guilds tended to locate in the
same areas. Some streets were named for the guilds
that they housed. Study street names in your community. Can you find reasons that particular names
were given to the streets in your neighborhood?

9. MR. WHO?

OBJECTIVE: Ap, An

As the craft guilds developed, so did many of our sir-
names. The makers of shoes became known as Shoemaker.
Silversmith, Baker and Weaver are other names that developed as a result of the trade of the family. Identify the sources of some of the names of your classmates.
Do you find any name that you believe originated from
the craft guilds? Explain your answer. The telephone
book is an excellent reference.

* 11. THE PEOPLE'S CHURCHES

OBJECTIVE: K, C, Ap

During the Middle Ages, Christians built beautiful
temples and cathedrals to honor their God. Make a
list of famous cathedrals built during the Middle
Ages. Try to find pictures of some. Make a display of famous cathedrals complete with information
about each.   You may also want to make a model of
one of the cathedrals.

13. RELIGIOUS CONFLICTS

OBJECTIVE: C

The crusades were directly associated with religion
and religious conflicts. However, the results of the
Crusades were far reaching and ultimately changed the
lives of most people in Europe. Crusaders were exposed to new products and luxuries of other lands. They
brought tales of their travels and stimulated the de-
mand for these new products. Soon buying and selling
increased and villages grew into towns and cities.
What were some of the products the Crusaders intro-
duced to the European people? How did these goods
change their lives?

15. SCHOOLS AND STUDY

OBJECTIVE: C, Ap

Education became important during this period. Compare education during the Renaissance with education
today. Who went to school? What did they study?
How were they taught? What other comparisons can
you make between the educational systems?

* 10. GOTHIC STYLE

OBJECTIVE: C, Ap, An

Gothic architecture became popular during the Middle
Ages. What are the characteristics of Gothic design?
Show examples by using pictures, arranged in a scrapbook and/or chart. Can you find examples of Gothic
architecture in your community? Photographs of these
buildings and their identifying details would be nice
to share in your presentation.

12. THEN AND NOW

OBJECTIVE: Ap, An

Compare merchant guilds and craft guilds to modern labor unions and fair trade commissions. What
similarities and differences do you find?

* 14. MEDIEVAL CITY

OBJECTIVE: Ap, An, S

Make a table top display or diorama to show what
life was like in a medieval city. You may base
your plan on the information in the book Trumpeter of Krakow.

16. RELIGIOUS LEADERSHIP

OBJECTIVE: C, E

While some religious leaders encouraged a split
with the Catholic church, others worked to improve and strengthen it. One of these was Ig-
natius Loyola. Investigate his work with a group
called the Jesuits. How did his work lead to a
stronger church? Why might Loyola be considered
a religious leader? Give reasons for your answer.

17. RELIGIOUS CHANGE

OBJECTIVE: C

People had new ideas about religion and the church, in the Middle Ages. Research the lives and works of Martin Luther and John Calvin. They were founders of the Protestant religions.

19. EARLY EXPLORERS

OBJECTIVE: K, C

The Renaissance was a time of exploration. Not only did people explore new ideas, but also new places. Complete the following chart to help you get an idea of the explorations into new regions.

Explorer	Exploration Date	Route	Native Country
Diaz			
Vasco de Gama			
Magellan			
Leif Ericson			

21. TALES OF RICHES

OBJECTIVE: C, An, S

The travels and tales of Marco Polo influenced Europeans. It might be interesting to research the life of this explorer to better understand his influence on the changes in European life. Write a diary telling of Marco Polo's adventures. You may also want to include maps of his journeys.

* 23. ON STAGE

OBJECTIVE: An, S

Columbus received aid from Queen Isabella and King Ferdinand of Spain. Create a drama in which Columbus seeks to convince the King and Queen of the worthiness of his venture. Be sure that reasons for the trip and Columbus' beliefs are evident to your audience. Make your drama as realistic as possible.

18. WORD STUDY

OBJECTIVE: K, C

Find the word Crusade in your dictionary. Explain the meaning in your own words. Now research the Crusades of the Middle Ages. What were they? Why were they organized? What success did they have?

20. THE DREAM

OBJECTIVE: C, An

Prince Henry of Portugal was intrigued with the riches of the East. He had a "sailor's dream." What was his plan? Did he see his dream come true? Was he right in his belief? Who actually carried out the dream of Prince Henry?

22. TRAVELS OF COLUMBUS

OBJECTIVE: C

Christopher Columbus was perhaps the most important explorer as far as our history is concerned. Find out about the life and travels of Columbus. Make a map to show his major voyages. Use different colors for each voyage. See how much information about Columbus you can find that is new to you.

24. AND THEN ....

OBJECTIVE: C, Ap

Make a time line. List all the major events you think are important through the Middle Ages. Arrange these events in order. Use illustrations for each event as well as a brief statement describing the event and the date.

25. THE AGE OF CHIVALRY

OBJECTIVE: Ap, An

The Renaissance gave rise to chivalry. What is chivalry today? Explain your answer.

* 27. CEREMONY AND SOCIETY

OBJECTIVE: C, An, S

Investiture ceremonies were held by kings during
the Middle Ages. What was involved in an Investiture Ceremony? What did the king actually do?
What affect did it have on others? How did Investiture help to change the status of the people?
How did this serve to change ways of life? Perhaps you will want to recreate an Investiture Ceremony.

29. THE COURTS

OBJECTIVE: K

In terms of the Middle Ages, define these:

> Trial by Ordeal
> Trial by Morsel
> Trial by Combat

Compare these systems for justice to our modern system.

* 31. CRIME AND PUNISHMENT

OBJECTIVE: An, S, E

Prepare a skit showing a "trial" during the Middle
Ages. You might also prepare a partner skit to
show how that same "crime" would be handled today.

26. PHILOSOPHY

OBJECTIVE: An, E

Humanism is an idealogy that emerged during the
Renaissance. We still hear much about humanism
today. What is the idea or theory of humanism?
What are the beliefs of the humanists? Is your
philosophy that of a humanist? Explain.

28. WHAT TO WEAR

OBJECTIVE: K, S

Fashions during the Renaissance were described
as flamboyant and gaudy. What do these terms
mean? Study the clothing of the people during
this time. Are these words good ones to describe this type of dress? Make a clothing scrapbook to show the dress of men and women during
the Renaissance. Include accessories as well as
garments.

30. TOOLS OF PUNISHMENT

OBJECTIVE: An, S, E

See if you can find out about various "tools"
used in punishment of a person judged guilty.
Make a chart to show such instruments. Give
the purpose of each.

32. JUSTICE?

OBJECTIVE: An, E

Consider Ordeal by Combat. What would happen today if we used this method of administering justice?
How would our lives be different? Do you think that
this was a fair means by which to punish people?
Support your answer with reasons.

33. MAPPING THE CRUSADES

OBJECTIVE: Ap

Draw a map of the route and/or the battles of the
First Crusades. Use different colors to indicate
the various routes and/or battles.

35. TABLE TOP MODELS

OBJECTIVE: Ap, S

Research in depth a particular battle or event
during the Crusades. Make a table top exhibit
to show the events you researched and to help
you explain what you have learned to others.

37. WORK TO DO

OBJECTIVE: An, E

Suppose you were living during the period of
the feudal system. What job would you want?
Give reasons for your answer.

39. JUDGMENT

OBJECTIVE: K, C

During the Middle Ages, there were no courts or
judicial systems as we know today. However, their
was crime and punishment. Find out how crimes were
punished. Who decided on guilt or innocence? On
what basis were these decisions made? What did
"bootles" mean? In your discussion of the judicial
system, explain these terms: mutilation, blinding,
felonies, and ducking stool.

34. ARMOR TYPES

OBJECTIVE: C, Ap

Soldiers of the Crusades representing various groups dressed in different armor. Draw a soldier representative of various groups. You might also want to model such dress by using dolls.

36. THE FEUDAL SYSTEM

OBJECTIVE: C, Ap

No study of the Middle Ages would be complete without some knowledge of the Feudal system. Read about it. Explain in your own words how it works. Include the advantages and disadvantages of such a system.

38. COMPARATIVE GOVERNMENTS

OBJECTIVE: Ap

Do you know of other governmental systems which would be like that of the feudal system? Make comparisons between those governmental systems you identify and the feudal system.

* 40. CASTLE PARTS

OBJECTIVE: K, C

During the Middle Ages, the wealthy lived in enormous homes called castles. There were hundreds of castles scattered around the countryside. Castles were built in different styles, but they shared many common features. Using a diagram or model, locate these areas of the castle and discuss their function:

well head	palisade	dungeon
outer bailey	bailey	fortress
forebuilding	bastion	lord
livery cupboard	treasury	moat

* 41. THE MANOR

OBJECTIVE: C, Ap, S

Plan, design and sketch, or build a diorama showing
a memorial village of feudal times. Include all areas of importance to its operation. Label each special area. You may want to make a tape recording to
tell about your plan and the areas you designated.

43. MANNERS

OBJECTIVE: C, Ap

Research "table manners." How do those accepted in
the Middle Ages differ from ours today? Which manners do we accept today which would have been unac-
ceptable during the Middle Ages? Is the reverse
true of any behaviors?

45. POACHING AND PENALTIES

OBJECTIVE: C, Ap

Poaching was prevalent during the Middle Ages. What
is it? Is there still poaching today? Do we have
laws to protect us from poaching? If so, what are
they? What were the penalties for poaching during
the Middle Ages?

47. HAWKS AND MAN

OBJECTIVE: C, An, E

Hawking was a form of sport. What is it? Do you
feel this would be an interesting sport? Could
you participate in hawking? Why or why not?

42. POSITION IN LIFE

OBJECTIVE: S

How would it feel to be a feudal serf? Write a
poem showing your feelings and emotions about
your state in life.

* 44. FEUDAL FOODS

OBJECTIVE: C, S

Find out about foods and food preparation. Plan
a dinner menu to be served at your castle. Be
sure it is in keeping with the times. You might
wish to prepare certain sample dishes for tasting.

* 46. TOURNAMENT PLAY

OBJECTIVE: C, S

Tournaments were the highlights of the lives of
the people. Describe a tournament. How was jousting learned? Prepare a skit demonstrating the art
of jousting. What other activities might you include in a tournament? Prepare an exhibit of a
tournament.

48. MAPPING THE WAY

OBJECTIVE: K, C, Ap

On an outline map show the Trade Routes of the Middle Ages. You might use symbols to show the products of particular geographic regions.

49. CELEBRATIONS

OBJECTIVE: C, Ap

Festivals which were important to the people were
Shrove Tuesdays, Palm Sunday, Whitaum, and Midsum-
mer Day. How were these celebrated? Which ones
of these do we still celebrate? How have the cel-
ebrations changed?

51. RENAISSANCE RECIPES

OBJECTIVE: C, Ap

Collect recipes from the Middle Ages and Renaissance. Put them together in your own Medieval
Recipe book or file.

53. STREET STORIES

OBJECTIVE: Ap

Study street maps of your town and perhaps maps
of other towns across the country. Locate street
names that may have originated long ago as the result of craft guilds.

55. BIOGRAPHY

OBJECTIVE: K, C

Research the life of printer-publisher John Gutenberg. What was his importance to the modern age?
What contribution to mankind did he make?

* 50. LIFE IN A CASTLE

OBJECTIVE: An, S

What was life in a castle like? Make a model of a castle and use puppets or dolls to show how the people lived. Have your "people" move about the castle as they might in their daily activities.

52. CHECKMATE

OBJECTIVE: C, Ap

The game of chess is a game of strategy with its roots based in the Middle Ages. Learn how to play the game. Plan a chess tournament. Perhaps you will want to schedule a life sized chess game. You and your classmates will be the pieces. Outline a giant chess board on the playground. Using simple costumes, define the "pieces" and play your best.

54. GOTHIC SCRAPBOOK

OBJECTIVE: Ap

Make a scrapbook to show examples of Gothic architecture from your community. Be sure that your illustrations show characteristic features. Caption each picture. Why do you think you might find Gothic influence in your community?

56. YOU! THE RULER

OBJECTIVE: An, S, E

You are the ruler of the manor. Select a name for yourself and your manor. Now write the laws for your serfs to obey. You may develop a skit to show how life on the manor would be living under your leadership.

Science & Math

SCIENCE & MATH

UNIT MATRIX

ACTIVITY	knowledge	Comprehension	Application	Analysis	Synthesis	Evaluation
1	X	X	X			
2	X	X			X	X
3	X	X	X			
4		X		X		X
5	X	X				
6	X	X				
7	X	X				
8		X		X		X
9	X	X		X		
10		X	X	·	X	
11		X	X			
12	X	X				
13				X		X
14		X		X		
15				X		X
16		X	X	X		
17	X	X		X		X
18	X			X		X
19		X		X		
20	X					
21	X	X				
22		X		X		
23			X		X	
24	X	X		X		X

Bloom's Taxonomy

1. SCIENTIFIC METHOD

OBJECTIVE: K, C, Ap

Science was an area that saw much change during the
surge of Renaissance thinking. The scientific method, which we use today, was developed. Make a chart
showing the steps in conducting a scientific investigation. Follow these steps to create a scientific
experiment. You, too, may make a scientific discovery.

* 3. EQUIPMENT

OBJECTIVE: K, C, Ap

Some of the important discoveries of the Renaissance
scientists were the litescope, the thermometer, the
microscope, and the clock. The appearance of these
tools have changed over the years. Find pictures of
these early examples of these instruments. Make drawings or sketches to show how each has changed. Has
the basic instrument remained the same?

5. SOLAR SYSTEM THEORY

OBJECTIVE: K, C

From the time of ancient Greece through the Middle Ages, people believed that the earth was fixed
in space and that all other heavenly bodies turned
around the earth. Renaissance science and a challenging Catholic priest proved this theory wrong.
Find out how this early scientist proved his theory.

7. HEALTH SCIENCES

OBJECTIVE: K, C

Attention was given to the study and understanding
of the human body. An English scientist discovered
that blood flows through the body. Who was this person? Give details about his discovery. How did this
information help mankind?

* 2. DISCOVERY

OBJECTIVE: K, C, S, E

Italian scientist Galileo is considered one of the founders of modern science. One of his most famous experiments was conducted from the Leaning Tower of Pisa. Describe the experiment. What did it prove? What scientific idea did it change? Develop a skit to show what you have learned.

4. EXPLOSIVES

OBJECTIVE: C, An, E

A Renaissance discovery to have a lasting impact on modern man was that of gun powder. When did gun powder first appear in Europe? Is there evidence that it may have come from another country? How did the use of gun powder change society? It is said that the use of gun powder in Europe put an end to feudalism and brought a beginning to a new way of living. Can you explain this statement?

* 6. MONTHS, DAYS AND YEARS

OBJECTIVE: K, C

A Renaissance "product" was our modern calendar. Find out about its development.

8. CHANGING IDEAS

OBJECTIVE: C, An, E

Inventions are created because men ask questions and challenge ideas. You have read about inventions during the Middle Ages that were the results of questioning minds. Can you think of modern inventions or discoveries that were made because men asked questions, studied the facts, and tried new ideas.

9. PET OR NOT?

OBJECTIVE: K, C, An

The Mastif is a breed of dog gaining popularity in America today. It was bred during the Middle Ages. It's power and speed could instantly separate a knight from his horse and snap the neck of a knight in full armour. Research this breed of dog. What characteristics does he have today that hint of his original breeding purpose?

* 11. BOOKKEEPING

OBJECTIVE: C, Ap

Fra Luca Pacioli is credited with the invention of the modern system of double entry bookkeeping. An accountant, store keeper, or perhaps your school secretary, can help you find information. Keep records of your spending using this technique.

13. MEDIEVAL DIET

OBJECTIVE: An, E

Study the diet of the people during the Middle Ages. Evaluate the common foods for nutritional value. Can you plan a wellbalanced medieval diet? Did these people eat junk food? Name some. You might prepare Medieval junk food to taste.

15. CHANGING BELIEFS

OBJECTIVE: An, E

What differences would we experience today if the beliefs and practices of the Middle Ages were still used by our physicians? How would this affect our lives? What differences might we expect in the way the world population has developed and changed? Would you prefer to be attended by a medicine man of the Middle Ages or a modern physician? Explain.

53

* 10. BANK OF THE TIMES

OBJECTIVE: C, Ap, S

Modern banking has its roots in the late Middle
Ages and early Renaissance. What can you learn
about the early banks and bankers? Medici is a
name of a banking family in Florence, Italy at
the time. You might start your study with him.
Compare banking during the Middle Ages with today. What has changed and what has remained the
same? Establish a bank of the times.

12. MEDIEVAL MEDICINE

OBJECTIVE: K, C

During the Middle Ages it was dangerous for schol-
ars and students to question old beliefs and suggest new knowledge or ideas. Read about medicine
at this time and write a factual report giving information about beliefs and practices. These terms
may help you in your understanding of this topic:
witchcraft, heresy, remedies, causes for illness,
barber, herbal healing, surgery, and Physic Garden.

* 14. HERBS AND HEALTH

OBJECTIVE: C, An

Herbal medicine was practiced at the time of the
Renaissance. What cultures today still practice
herbal medicine? Can you find any traditions or
customs that can be traced to the belief in herbs
and treatments and cures? Plant you own herbal
gardens. Study the varieties of plants. (Do NOT
practice your own medicine!)

16. LIFE EXPECTANCY

OBJECTIVE: C, Ap, An

Investigate the famous people mentioned in this
study. Make a chart to show birthdate, death
date, and age of each. Find the average life
span for these people. Compare the life span of
the Middle Ages to ours today. What generaliza-
tions can you make?

17. ASTRONOMY

OBJECTIVE: K, C, An, E

Copernicus was much interested in the earth's movement and its relationship to other heavenly bodies. He studied Ptolemy's theory. His observations were in conflict. Explain the theories of these two scientists.

19. DREADED DISEASE

OBJECTIVE: C, An

Leprosy was a dreadful disease during this period. Research the disease. Consider its history, treatment, and current status. Compare and contrast attitudes toward leprosy then and today. Keep your report factual.

21. WRITING MATERIALS

OBJECTIVE: K, C

Parchment and vellum were materials used for writing then, much as we use paper now. What were these made of? Discuss the process involved in preparing them for use.

23. LONG, HARD RIDE

OBJECTIVE: Ap, S

If a single horseman rode from sunup to sundown, he would travel 36 miles. How long would it take to travel 156 miles? Remember to travel in daylight. Make some other story problems based on this information for others to solve.

18. PRESERVING FOOD

OBJECTIVE: K, An, E

Food preservation was a problem during the Middle Ages. What were the processes used in order to preserve food? What were the advantages and disadvantages of each process? What problems did food preservation create for the medieval individual? How did these problems effect the diet during this period?

20. AMAZING PREDICTIONS

OBJECTIVE: K

Roger Bacon was keenly interested in the secrets held by nature. He believed that through observation and experimentation, man could learn much. Investigate his life and work. Bacon made some predictions about future scientific developments that have come true. What were his predictions, particularly regarding development in the area of transportation?

22. ASTROLOGY

OBJECTIVE: C, An

People at this time believed that their lives were controlled by the stars. Astrology was used to determine dates for coronations and other important events. Research the science of astrology.

24. WEIGHTS AND MEASURES

OBJECTIVE: K, C, An, E

Weight and measurement was important to the alchemist. Discuss the tools used. What standardization was there in these measures? Why is standardization important?

Art & Music

ART & MUSIC

UNIT MATRIX

ACTIVITY	knowledge	Comprehension	Application	Analysis	Synthesis	Evaluation
1		X	X			
2					X	
3				X	X	
4				X	X	
5	X	X			X	
6					X	
7				X	X	
8	X	X			X	
9					X	
10	X	X				
11					X	
12	X	X			X	
13	X	X			X	
14				X	X	
15	X	X	X		X	
16	X	X	X		X	
17	X	X			X	
18	X	X				
19			X	X	X	
20		X			X	
21	X	X			X	
22				X	X	
23		X			X	
24		X			X	

Bloom's Taxonomy

1. SECULAR SONGS

OBJECTIVE: C, Ap

Music during the Middle Ages grew more secular in nature. What does secular mean? What is secular music? Is popular music today secular? Give examples of secular music, and examples of music that is not secular in nature. How do they compare?

* 3. TRAVELING TROUBADOURS

OBJECTIVE: An, S

Who were the troubadours? What did they contribute to the lives of the people during the Middle Ages? Pretend you are a troubadour. Develop an act that demonstrates the life and work of a troubadour.

5. INTERVIEWING THE CRAFTSMAN

OBJECTIVE: K, C, S

Colored or stained glass windows were popular during the Middle Ages and are still popular today. Someone in your community may teach the art of making stained glass. You may find listings for such classes in the telephone book. Try to interview the teacher of such a class. Find the steps necessary to create stained glass pictures. There are also some dangers and special problems to consider. Be sure to think out your questions carefully before you interview your craftsman. Share information you receive with the class.

* 7. FASHION DESIGN

OBJECTIVE: An, S

Costumes and clothing were quite elaborate and at the same time quite simple. Sketch or design clothing of the barons, clergy, knights, burgess, and peasant. Make finger puppets to use in an original puppet show. Dress your puppets authentically.

2. PERSONALITY SHIELD

OBJECTIVE: S

On an outline of a knight's shield, show a design
that would be representative of you. Consider your
personality, likes; dislikes, etc. Create your shield
so that it is uniquely yours.

* 4. THE "OLD" YOU!

OBJECTIVE: An, S

Make a costume for yourself, characteristic of the
period. You might develop a crest or coat of arms
on your tunic. Use crayons to create the design.
Then place the fabric between two sheets of paper
and iron. This gives your design a finished look.
You may want to create your own design on an old
shirt or a T-shirt.

* 6. STAINED GLASS COPIES

OBJECTIVE: S

You can make copies of stained glass windows by using simple materials. Draw the pattern of your window on heavy paper. Cut out the figures and sections
needing color. Leave the heavy paper only to outline
and hold pieces together. Paste colored paper behind
the heavy paper to give the proper colors in each area.
Hang your tissue paper window in a real window so that
the light shines through. It will give the appearance
of stained glass. You may want to create windows of
your own or reproduce a pattern of the Middle Ages that
you like.

8. KNIGHT PICTURES

OBJECTIVE: K, C, S

Draw a knight in full armor. Label the parts.

9. PRINT IT YOURSELF

OBJECTIVE: S

Block printing was not only an art form, but also
the only way of reproducing books other than copy-
ing by hand before the time of printing presses.
Discover how a block print can be made. Using the
block print technique, make your own book. You may
want to choose a simple picture book for young chil-
dren. Keep your designs simple. Being able to make
more than one copy is an advantage of block printing.

11. MAKING A MINI-MUSEUM

OBJECTIVE: S

You may want to join with other classmates who have
studied other Renaissance artists. Perhaps you will
want to develop a mini-museum to display reproductions
of the work of these famous artists. Conduct tours
through your mini-museum.

* 13. DANCE! DANCE! DANCE!

OBJECTIVE: K, C, S

Perhaps you can investigate the dance of the times.
Maybe your town has dance teams or teachers who can
help you learn some Renaissance dances. As you study
the style you may develop a dance of your own, with
similar characteristics.

* 15. SING A SONG

OBJECTIVE: K, C, Ap, S

Wandering minstrels roamed the countryside singing their ballads. Find out what a ballad is.
Perhaps you can learn some ballads to share. Maybe you will even want to write your own ballad.

10. RENAISSANCE ARTISTS

OBJECTIVE: K, C

Many famous artists emerged during the Renaissance.
Some of these were Michelangelo, Raphael, and Leonardo da Vinci. Investigate the life and works of
one of these artists. Prepare a biography to tell
about the artist and his life. Also collect pictures of the works of the artist. Make a display
to show what you have learned. Each of these artists had other skills as well, highlight these.

* 12. THE PERFORMERS

OBJECTIVE: K, C, S

Every lady and gentlemen was expected to know and
be able to perform music. They amused themselves
by singing and playing. Some of the instruments
of the time were virginals, lutes, and violas.
What did they look like? Use pictures and diagrams
to help explain. Are these instruments still used
today? What sound did they make? Can you reproduce
a musical instrument like those in the Middle Ages?
Perhaps you and several others can demonstrate your
musical instruments by playing together.

* 14. COPY THE STYLE

OBJECTIVE: An, S

Study the style of the great masters of Renaissance
art. Try your hand at painting pictures in this style.
Mat and/or frame your pictures and develop your own Renaissance Art Show.

* 16. THE JUGGLER

OBJECTIVE: K, C, Ap, S

Juggling might be considered an art form. Can you
explain why? Juggling was a popular sport during
this time. Try your hand at juggling. If you are
really good, you may want to develop an act as a
juggler to share with others.

* 17. SAND CASTING

OBJECTIVE: K, C, S

What is sand casting? How is this process done?
Sand casting was a method used for producing art-
icles in the Middle Ages. Try your hand at sand
casting.

19. LISTEN AND LEARN

OBJECTIVE: Ap, An, S

Ask your music teacher to help you locate records
and music representative of the time. Listen to
the music. Compare and contrast it to our music
today. Try your hand at producing a piece of Middle Ages music.

21. PARTS OF THE WHOLE

OBJECTIVE: K, C, S

Draw a diagram of a knight in full armor as he
might look in the year 2050. Consider the size,
special problems, reasons for armor, etc.

23. TAPESTRY ART

OBJECTIVE: C, S

What is tapestry art? Choose a medieval design that
you think might be found on a tapestry of the Middle
Ages. Create your design by drawing or painting it
on fabric to make a wall hanging. Consider the style,
design, texture, and colors.

18. THE MAN IN THE MUSIC

OBJECTIVE: K, C

"The Man of La Mancha" is a modern story about the famous Don Quixote. Listen to the theme song "Impossible Dream." Outline the story from the lyrics.

* 20. COSTUME MURAL

OBJECTIVE: C, S

Make a costume scrapbook or mural. Show the dress of various groups of people during the Middle Ages. Use diagrams to show samples of this periods costumes. Also include brief descriptions. You may want to costume dolls instead of using drawings. Perhaps you can arrange your dolls with scenic backgrounds as they would be in a museum. Label each part of your display.

22. MEDIEVAL MASCOT

OBJECTIVE: An, S

Do you have a school symbol and/or mascot? If so, give it a "Middle Ages" look. Redesign the basic symbol showing the artistic flair of the times. If you don't have one, create your own school symbol. Maybe you could conduct a contest!

* 24. REPRODUCE THE SOUND

OBJECTIVE: C, S

Use recorders and other simple instruments to re-create a medieval concert. Choose authentic ballads and tunes. Then perhaps you will want to write one of your own using the same style.